Festival of Awkward Moments:
The Anthology
2011
Freshwater Theatre

A Festival of Awkward Moments was produced by Freshwater Theatre in May 2011 at the Gremlin Theatre in St. Paul, Minnesota, with the directors and casts:

Diarrhea by Dawson Moore, directed by Jimmy LeDuc
Featuring Josh Carson and Courtney Miner

A Little Nightmare Before Christmas by Persephone Vandegrift, directed by Ryan Henderson
Featuring Neal Beckman, Bob Flynn, Addie Phelps and Renata Shaffer-Gottschalk

Halitosis by Roger Brookfield, directed by Scott Pakudaitis
Featuring Kate Gunther and Matthew Saxe

Old MacDonald Dirge by Justin Maxwell, directed by Derek Ewing
Featuring Brigid Kelly

Dream Sequence by Scot Moore, directed by John Leaf
Featuring Brian Casey and John Leaf

Strings by J. Merrill Motz, directed by Katie Starks
Featuring Kendra Ryan and Josh Vogen

Wingman by Eric "Pogi" Sumangil, directed by Derek Ewing
Featuring Brigid Kelly and Josh Carson

Time In by James Reynolds, directed by Ariel Pinkerton
Featuring Katie Starks and Charla Lange

Bedtime Story by Valerie Borey, directed by Edward Linder
Featuring Rick Logan, Stacey Poirer and Mame Pelletier

Flapjacks & Bagels by Mame Pelletier, directed by Ben Layne
Featuring Amber Bjork, Geoffrey Hofman-Frethem, Victoria Pyan and Adan Varela

Cut or Uncut by Neil Haven, directed by Amber Bjork
Featuring D.L. Diltz, Megan Engeseth, Brian Hesser, Ben Layne and Mikey Wadlund

Pet Names by Stacey Lane, directed by Jimmy LeDuc
Featuring Josh Carson and Courtney Miner

Mr. Gingersnap by Nichole Carey, directed by David Schlosser
Featuring Mark Mattison, David McMenomy and Kyra Corrine Warren

No Goat by Ruth Virkus, directed by Ben Layne
Featuring Amber Bjork and Geoffrey Hofman-Frethem

Freshwater Theatre would like to thank the brave, beautiful and bold theatre community of the Twin Cities.

TABLE OF CONTENTS

DIARRHEA BY DAWSON MOORE	7
PET NAMES BY STACEY LANE	10
A LITTLE NIGHTMARE BEFORE YOUR CHRISTMAS BY PERSEPHONE VANDEGRIFT	14
TIME IN BY JAMES REYNOLDS	19
DREAM SEQUENCE BY SCOT MOORE	27
BEDTIME STORY BY VALERIE BOREY	30
HALITOSIS BY ROGER BROOKFIELD	39
MR. GINGERSNAP BY NICHOLE CAREY	45
WINGMAN BY ERIC "POGI" SUMANGIL	56
FLAPJACKS AND BAGELS BY MAME PELLETIER	62
STRINGS BY J. MERRILL MOTZ	68
OLD MACDONALD DIRGE BY JUSTIN MAXWELL	76
CUT OR UNCUT BY NEIL HAVEN	79
NO GOAT BY RUTH VIRKUS	89

Please Note: Freshwater Theatre retains no rights to the following scripts. If you wish to produce any of the following scripts, please contact the authors. Contact information for all playwrights or their agents directly precedes each script in this anthology.

The more local something is, the more it is universal. - Joan Miro

www.freshwatertheatre.com

Our Mission:

We believe that art comes from a place. And we believe, unapologetically, that our place is one of the very best. We exist not only to create our own theater, but to facilitate and promote a vision of the Twin Cities as a major exporter of performing arts. We do beautiful, brave work here. This is an artistic community of revelation, innovation and pride. We have big dreams for **Freshwater Theatre Company**, and that includes this entire community of artists, individually and collectively.

Founded by the husband and wife team of Ben Layne and Ruth Virkus, with the help of fantastic colleagues and friends, **Freshwater Theatre Company's** motto is simple: we love good stories, told simply and told well. We believe that theatre can be transformative, revelatory, and educational, but we love it best when it's a good time, too. We like to entertain, and we promise a helluva ride.

We refuse to apologize or compromise. It's time to get serious, Twin Cities. This isn't flyover country. We're a coast, too. In fact, we have more coastline in Minnesota than anywhere else in the United States. The water is just fresher here.

Freshwater Theatre. We're in it for all of us.

Diarrhea

By Dawson Moore
Please contact him at dawsonguy@juno.com

Dawson Moore is an award-winning playwright, director, teacher, and actor. He works for Prince William Sound Community College in Valdez, Alaska, as the Coordinator of their Playwriting AFA degree and the Last Frontier Theatre Conference. His plays have been produced in around the country and internationally. He has won national playwriting awards for his short comedies *The Peach, Burning, The Bus, Bile in the Afterlife,* and *Domestic Companion.* The companies who have staged his work include TBA Theatre, Kokopelli Theatre Company, Theatre Artists Conspiracy, Three Wise Monkeys, Unidentified Theatre Company, Reston Community Players, Impact Theatre, Bellingham Theatre Guild, UAA Theatre & Dance, Circle East, Fairbanks Drama Association, Eccentric Theatre Company, Bradley University, Prince William Sound Community College, Eureka Theatre Company, Expanded Arts Theatre, 78th Street Studio Theatre, Las Positas College, Theatro del Naville, Isis Arts Collective, Nearly Stellar Entertainment, Love Creek Productions, Playwrights Center of San Francisco, Venue 9, TOAST, the Rough Theatre Company, Two Spoons Theatre Company, Northwest Playwrights Alliance, Theatre Limina, Alleyway Theatre, Circus Theatricals, Salt City Artists League, Theare Daedelus, Java Theatre, the University of Idaho, Blue Roses and the Mid-America Theatre Conference. His other plays include *LibidOFF*; *Happy Loving Couples are a Thing of the Past*; *Secret Stuffing*; *Alyson and the Great Bagel Mistake*; *The Fears of Harold Shivvers*; *Living with the Savage*; *Oh, Nancy!*; *In a Red Sea*; *Laundry Day*; *Love's Lumberings Remembered*; *Skid Marks*; *The Tie*; *Six Dead Bodies Duct-Taped to a Merry-Go-Round;* and *The War of Virginia and Alabama.*

Production History
Diarrhea was previously produced as a part of the 3rd Annual DNA Festival of Very Very Very Short Plays at the University of Idaho.

Peter and Lisa sit next to each other on a couch. Dance music and party sounds are in the background.

PETER
So… uh…

LISA
What?

PETER
I wanted to ask you to… some thing… at some time… but I can't remember either of the details.

LISA
Well, then I guess I'm not sure if I'm free then, or if I want to do that.

PETER
But when I ask you out, I don't want you to get the wrong idea. It would be presumptuous, at least, if not outright rude, for me to ask you on a date. The embarrassment. I just wouldn't do it. I can't imagine dealing with the look in your eyes, that "oh-how-sad" look. And say you did say you'd go out with me on a date-date if I asked you, that would be even worse. The debate about whether to bring flowers, write a poem, cologne, tie… a million questions and worries. And really, only the possibility of falling short of what an amazing woman like you needs. Smart and sexy and funny and talented and kind. You're a taller order than I can fill. And what would I do if we went out and you made a move on me? If I did nothing, and you leaned across my gearshift to kiss me. I'd open my car door and fall to the cold earth and thank God. Or curse God. Whichever, it'd be odd behavior and it'd turn you off and weird you out and then you wouldn't want to be my friend and let me look at you. I love the way you look. Your appearance alone makes me smile. Your smile makes me glow inside, makes me warm, makes me happy all over my entire body. Or maybe you're really more like a barium enema, because I know that you will inevitably hurt me and give me diarrhea. I'm… just kidding there. Romance doesn't really give me diarrhea. Only on the really bad days. And you're getting out of a, what, five-year relationship? The only feeling I can imagine exceeding the joy of having your love would be the devastation of losing it. "Better to have tried and failed than never to risked at all," or whatever that phrase is, fucking ridiculous. Especially if the failing comes over and over and over again at the same thing. That's just being bullheaded,

and I'm not bullheaded about romance with beautiful women. I'm really trying to shop for something more in my league. Something more desperate and fucked up. And not beautiful like you. You can't help but destroy me, and I want to spare you that guilt. So, do you want to go see that play on Friday? I hear it's good.

LISA
No, actually, you're a little weird for me right now, even without talking to

God. I have to go. My boyfriend's over there… we didn't break up.

She leaves. He exhales deeply.

PETER
Whew.

End of play.

PET NAMES
© 2011
StaceyLaneInk@yahoo.com
www.StaceyLaneInk.com

Stacey Lane's plays have been seen at over two-hundred theatres from coast to coast in the U.S., as well as in Canada, England, and Australia and are published with Playscripts, Inc., Smith and Kraus, Manhattan Theatre Source, San Luis Obispo Little Theatre, and Scene4 Magazine. She is the recipient of the Helene Wurlitzer Foundation Residency Grant, the Montgomery County Arts & Cultural District's Literary Artist Fellowship, a "Charlie Award", and a nominee for "Outstanding Playwriting for a New Script of a Play or Book of a Musical" at the Midtown International Theatre Festival.

PRODUCTION HISTORY

Spare Change Theatre NYC, NY	In a New York Minute June 2010
Artist's Showcase of Atlanta Atlanta, GA	Production Aug. 2010
Gateway Film Center Columbus, OH	Frogs with Fangs May 2011
Freshwater Theatre Co. Minneapolis, MN	Festival of Awkward Moments May 2011

Cast of Characters

Brenda: The wife

Nelson: The husband

Scene

The Easter Bunny's photo station at the mall (can be represented by a bare stage).

Time

Spring.

SETTING: The Easter Bunny's photo station at the mall.

AT RISE: BRENDA and NELSON face the unseen Easter Bunny. NELSON is snapping pictures with his camera.

BRENDA
Look at Daddy, sweetheart.

NELSON
Over here!
(He takes a picture.)

BRENDA
She wasn't looking.

NELSON
Of course she's not looking. She's terrified.

BRENDA
There's nothing to be afraid of, doll baby. Mommy is right here. The Easter Bunny is nice. Be a good girl and Mommy will give you a special treat.

NELSON
(Snapping a photo.)
Got it.

BRENDA
Her eyes were closed. Take another.

NELSON
Look at the long line. I think we're done here.

BRENDA
We waited in that long line and now it is our turn. All of our friends can't wait to see how big Mommy's little angel is getting. Don't stick out your tongue like that, honey.

NELSON
(Taking another photo.)
That one was a keeper. Now let's go.

BRENDA
Give the Easter Bunny a kiss, lovey. Wouldn't that be cute?

NELSON
I don't-

BRENDA
Oh! I don't think the Easter Bunny wants to be licked there, angel!

NELSON
Oh shit! I think she just peed on the Easter Bunny.

BRENDA

He's a professional. He can take it.

NELSON
This was clearly a bad idea.

BRENDA
One more picture.

NELSON
The bunny is covered in piss.

BRENDA
You can Photoshop out the urine stain. Look at me! Who's Mommy's precious princess? Oh, sweetie! Please stop humping the Easter Bunny's leg.

NELSON
Bad dog!

(BLACKOUT)

A Little Nightmare Before Your Christmas

Persephone Vandegrift
214 Summit Ave E #102
Seattle, WA 98102
Persephone.v.writes@gmail.com

Persephone Vandegrift presently resides ~~in the Underworld~~ in Seattle and is absolutely thrilled to be included in Freshwater Theatre's Awkward Moments festival and anthology.

Along with *A Little Nightmare Before Your Christmas*, she is the author of several short plays: *It's a Classic, Return of Helen, The Ticket, It's Not Really Suicide, Is It?, Ileya,* and full-length adaptation of The Bacchae of Euripides called *Revenge and Sorrow in Thebes*. Most recently she has been working on an anthology of poems and short stories based on Greek and Celtic mythology titled *When Apollo Closes a Door, He Opens Too Many Windows* as well as another full-length stage play *These Women of Myth and Circumstance*.

Besides an incurable addiction for ancient history and mythology, Seph has also made the leap into film-script writing and presently has 2 feature scripts under her belt; *Death of a Mortal Woman* and *The Curse of Mercy Wood* along with short scripts *Santa's Last Stand* and *All Things Hidden*.

Her children's book *The Maiden Tree* is under publishing consideration. She is currently represented by the Jenée Arthur Agency LLC. For more information about Seph's writing (and feel free to hire her as a writer so that she can quit her day job), please pop on over to her website www.flyingelfproductions.webs.com or pay a visit to www.jeneearthuragency.com/arthurs-authors/persephone-vandegrift

A living room.

In the half-light, a man dressed in full Santa suit enters. He takes a few presents out of a bag and puts them under a make-shift Christmas tree.

Wendy enters in her lingerie; she's a bit tipsy. She is gripping an empty wine bottle.

WENDY:
(*shouting behind her, laughing*)
I'm jus' getting it...calm down! I'll be back in a sec. Crap, I can't see.

She slaps at the light-switch or haphazardly manages to turn on a nearby lamp. As the lights go to full, she turns and sees Santa.

WENDY:
Ohmygod!

SANTA:
Wendy?

WENDY:
Dad?

Wendy grabs the cover off the armrest or sofa whatever piece of fabric is nearest to her and holds it over her chest.

WENDY:
What are you doing here? How'd you get in?

DAD:
I just finished my shift at Macy's. And you gave me a set of keys, remember?

WENDY:
Yeah, but not to use them!

DAD:
Well, I wanted to make Christmas a little special for you this year. And I thought you said you wouldn't be back until tomorrow.

Rebecca stumbles in, very drunk, in her lingerie.

REBECCA:
Hey sweetie, what's taking so long? Santa?

WENDY:
Oh God.

REBECCA:
(*kisses Wendy*)
Awww lover, you wanted to surprise me! Santa, what did you bring me?

Simon staggers in, also drunk, in his boxers. Dad isn't sure what to make of it all. Wendy is a deer in headlights.

SIMON:
(*loudly*)
OMG lol. Staaaanta!

REBECCA:
(*smacks Simon in chest*)
<u>Santa</u> - god you are so drunk!

WENDY:
Rebecca...stop...

REBECCA:
(*to Simon*)
And why are you out of bed? We didn't give you permission to...

WENDY:
Shhhh...

REBECCA:
Why? Shhh...you. And where's the wine? Santa needs some wine.

SIMON:
Hey Santa?

SANTA:
Yes, my son?

SIMON:
Ohhh a proper Santa...hey...hey...where's the sleigh?

WENDY:
Simon...stop. Please.

SIMON:
And the sexy elvish women.

SANTA:
(*playing along, disguising his voice*)
Oh hohohoho, now Simon, you've got some fine ones right here m'boy. Don't go...ah...wishin'...making wishes...

SIMON:
Santa's Irish?

Rebecca and Simon start laughing at themselves, hysterically.

WENDY:
Okay sooo Santa, are you finished with your Santa stuff for tonight?

DAD:
I sure am there...little girl. Have millions of other houses to get to...

WENDY:
I bet you do so let me walk you out.

Santa starts to leave, Wendy follows, placing a firm hand on his back.

REBECCA:
Noooo make him use the chimney like all the
other Santas!

DAD:
Now, now Reb...you...little naughty girl...what comes down doesn't always have to go up! Uh, well, never mind! A ho ho ho everybody!

Rebecca and Simon look at each other, confused, and then start laughing again.

WENDY:
Dad...I...

DAD:

Now, Santa says for you all to stay safe and tucked up inside your beds tonight! All right?

Simon gives Santa some sort of 'peace out' or 'brotherhood' type of wave.

SIMON:
Yes sir, Santa! You're the man!

DAD:
(*in his own voice*)
No, Simon. I definitely think <u>you're</u> the man here tonight.

Dad gives Wendy a stern look, hands her back her keys, and exits.

REBECCA:
Bye Santa!

SIMON:
I love you Santa!

Beat. Rebecca stares at Simon.

SIMON:
I do...I love Santa.

REBECCA:
Okay, I give up sweetheart. Who was that Santa?

Wendy turns to them carefully, half-smiling.

WENDY:
Well, you guys, that - was my father.

Lights fade on the sheer horror of it hits Simon and Rebecca. Rebecca's hand instinctively goes up to cover her cleavage as the smile fades from Simon's face.

THE END

Time In
Copyright © 2011 by James Reynolds

James Reynolds
2459 La Costa Avenue
Chula Vista, CA 91915
(619) 482-8687
jarreynolds@hotmail.com

James Reynolds is novice playwright despite being in his sixties. Jim just started writing plays last year. So far he has written only comedies, everything from one-minute to full-length plays. Time In is his first play to be produced onstage anywhere, for which he is grateful to the Freshwater Theatre for being the first to showcase an unknown.

Jim has a Bachelors Degree in Architecture from Rensselaer Polytechnic Institute and a MBA from UCLA. He served as an Army Lieutenant in Vietnam. He made his living as a Registered Architect at private architectural firms and public agencies in the states of New York, Washington, and California.

In his spare time back in the 60's, 70's, and 80's, Jim acted in and/or did set design for over 30 plays in various community theaters in upstate New York and the Seattle area. From time to time, he made sporadic attempts at writing plays, but found it frustrating to do so using a typewriter (remember those?) When he got married and had a family in the mid-80's, he stopped having the free time to do theater.

Now that he is a retired architect and we have computers for the painstaking work of re-writing, he has revived a lifelong urge to be a playwright. Jim lives with his wife Mary in the San Diego suburb of Chula Vista.

CAST OF CHARACTERS
[2 females]

SHARLENE — White woman in her 30's.

KEZIAH — Afro-American woman in her 30's.

TIME

A weekday in the present.

SETTING

The inside of an elevator cab, suggested by the corners and edges of a rectangular box about 6 feet by 6 feet horizontally by 8 feet vertically, plus horizontal lines on the back and two sides at 3 feet above the floor to suggest handrails, and a small square solid panel at one front corner about 3 feet above the floor to suggest the elevator control panel.

(SHARLENE is standing in the middle of the elevator cab. KEZIAH is waiting outside the elevator. SHARLENE mimes being jostled by the elevator stopping at a floor, followed by the sounds of a "ding" and the elevator doors opening. SHARLENE sees KEZIAH and moves all the way to one back corner of the elevator, clutching her shoulder purse closer. KEZIAH enters the elevator and moves to the other back corner. The sound of the elevator doors closing and more mimed jostling indicates that the elevator has begun moving. SHARLENE takes a cell phone out of her purse, can't get a connection, but pretends she did and fakes a conversation.)

SHARLENE

Yes, dear! How are things down at the police station? No, I haven't had a chance to try out my new taser gun yet, but I do have it with me, all charged up just like you said. But really, why do I even need it? I never carry any cash on me. Or credit cards. Why on earth would I want to make it worthwhile for anyone to rob me? Anyway, if anything should happen, I just thought I'd call from the elevator farthest from the front doors in the Alexander Hamilton Building to say how much I love you. Bye. (Hangs up.)

KEZIAH
Surprisingly good reception from inside an elevator. (No response.) Kind of a rickety old elevator, isn't it? Feel how slowly it's moving?

SHARLENE
The same thought occurred to me.

KEZIAH
I hope it's been inspected sometime in the past decade. What do you think?

SHARLENE
I have no idea how often elevators are supposed to be inspected.

KEZIAH
I didn't really think you did. I was just making conversation.

SHARLENE
Strangers are not supposed to talk to each other in the elevator.

KEZIAH
Is that some rule according to the Geneva Convention for Prisoners of Elevators?

SHARLENE
"Prisoner"? Even now, you still think of yourself as a prisoner?

KEZIAH
"Still"?

SHARLENE
Still, you think of us as prisoners in this elevator?

KEZIAH
Oh yeah, us prisoners. No, I don't think of us as prisoners. Most people don't get my sense of humor. That's alright. I'm not offended.

SHARLENE

Oh, OK. I understand. I'm a sympathetic person at heart. I know how things are, out in the world. We didn't all get to go to the finest schools. You shouldn't be too hard on yourself. I'm sure you have many fine qualities which nobody even suspects, myself included. Especially since I'll bet you only made it through-- what grade?

KEZIAH (Counting to herself.)
Nineteenth?

SHARLENE
No dear, there is no such thing as nineteenth grade. Perhaps you meant ninth grade?

KEZIAH
You're right. There is no nineteenth grade. I forgot that you stop numbering after high school. I should have said instead, "Post-Doctoral". I have a Ph.D. in sociology.

SHARLENE
Oh my, that's very good of you. Surprisingly good, considering.

KEZIAH
"Considering" what?

SHARLENE
Considering . . . how we women have been held back for so long.

KEZIAH
Mercy, me! You know it's been an uphill struggle for us womenfolk!

SHARLENE
Preach it, Sister!

KEZIAH
I feel so close to you now. Want a hug?

SHARLENE
(Tries to back away but there's no room.)
The reason you feel so close is because it's so cramped here in this tiny elevator. But that's really great news about all your college degrees. You should be proud of yourself. (*pause*) Where did you attend college?

KEZIAH
Brown.

SHARLENE
(Referring to the color brown.)
"Brown", of course! Where else?

KEZIAH
(Pretending she had meant "At what other school?")
Columbia.

SHARLENE
The country?

KEZIAH
The university.

SHARLENE
The University of Colombia? Weren't you extremely uncomfortable down there being around that dictator Hugo Chavez?

KEZIAH
Even if I had attended the National University of Colombia in Bogota rather than Columbia University in New York, I would not have been in the same country as Hugo Chavez. He's the president of Venezuela.

(A loud grinding sound and the severe jostling of BOTH passengers indicate that the elevator has abruptly stopped between floors.)

SHARLENE
Oh, no. We're stuck between floors. Why did that happen? You're the one with all the education.

KEZIAH
Not in elevator maintenance. How about a 9-1-1 call on your cell?

SHARLENE
No, my cell phone won't work in here. *(Pause.)* Because it ran out of charge at the end of my last conversation to my husband, the policeman.

KEZIAH
That explains everything. I see there's an "Emergency" button to push.
(Pushes it.)

SHARLENE
I'll bet it's not even connected to anything.

KEZIAH
I'll let that pessimistic comment pass because you're anxious. Possibly claustrophobic?

SHARLENE
(*Panicky.*)
Oh, God! I forgot all about that!

KEZIAH
I need to edit my comments better. Do you have any Valium in your purse?

SHARLENE
(*Breathing hard.*)
Well, of course. But I'm not just going to hand them over to you. Get your own drugs.
You must know plenty of dealers.

KEZIAH
I was thinking you should take one yourself. Maybe two.

SHARLENE
(*Fishing the bottle out of her purse.*)
I have three.

KEZIAH
Knock yourself out. Please.

SHARLENE
(*Wolfing down the pills.*)
You're the doctor. Not actually a Medical Doctor, but the only doctor we have in this cramped tiny little hot airless box with no earthly way out!

KEZIAH
Sharlene, listen. Take deep breaths of cool, fresh air and tell yourself to "Re-laxxxx".

SHARLENE
(*Shouting.*)
RE-LAXXXX !

KEZIAH
Use your Indoor Voice.

SHARLENE
(Shouting even louder.)
IN-DOOR ?

KEZIAH
Shhhh. Shhhh. Re-laxxx. Re-laxxx. (*SHARLENE calms down.*)
Much better. Dr. Keziah approves.

SHARLENE
"Keziah"? What is that? Some sort of African name that means "Worth Many Goats" in Swahili?

KEZIAH
Hebrew. From the Bible.

KEZIAH
Keziah was a daughter of Job. Her name is associated with female equality because she is one of the rare women in the Bible to receive an equal portion of her father's inheritance with her brothers. That's why my mother named me after her.

SHARLENE
OK, sermon's over. What really matters is that I 'm feeling much better after your little Bible story distracted me. Plus the drugs kicked in. You know, for a sociologist you're a pretty good doctor.

KEZIAH
Whenever we do get out of this elevator, you might be a little too "relaxed" to drive. Want me to drop you off at the bunker on my way home to the 'Hood?

SHARLENE
NO! Owww! All of a sudden, I don't feel so well, in my tummy. Wait a minute. Those weren't Valium I took. I remember now. I was re-using this empty Valium bottle for some other pills. But if they weren't Valium, what were they? They must have been . . . oh, no.

KEZIAH
What? Tell me what you took.

SHARLENE
Colon detox!

KEZIAH
High-powered laxatives?

SHARLENE and KEZIAH (In unison.)
NOOOOOOOOOOOOOO!

(BLACKOUT.   End of play.)

Dream Sequence
Scot Moore
scotmoore@gmail.com

Scot Moore graduated from UW-River Falls with a degree in Theatre and Broadcast Journalism and has since worked in theatre as an actor, director, producer, and designer for 15 years. He's also a playwright and musician and is very happy to lend his many hats to Freshwater Theatre. As an actor, he's worked with Starting Gate, Theatre in the Round, Bedlam Theatre, Nimbus Theatre, Epic Arts Repertory Theatre, Commedia Beauregard, Cromulent Shakespeare Co, Way to Go Turbo, and more.

For the next two years, Scot will be dedicating all his theatrical free time to the production end of Freshwater while he undergoes a lengthy process of minor facial reconstruction (it's a long story). This leaves lots of time to get things done, including directing Freshwater's next show, *The Book of Liz*, which runs this September at the new Nimbus Theater in Minneapolis!

For more about Scot, and for samples of his writing, please visit:
www.scotmoore.net

ARTHUR – A nervous, somewhat disturbed man. Has had a troubling dream.
ROGER – A married man.

> *(At rise, ARTHUR is pacing Center. He speaks to himself throughout until the very end. A park bench or chair can be used if necessary)*

ARTHUR

I had a dream about your wife, Roger. She let me do awful things to her. Awful... *(He trails off, debating the meaning of "awful")* Well, awful's subjective I guess. I guess... Is it wrong to think of someone's wife in a way that makes him think that what he's doing is... awful? Awful.

(He now goes into a suave, storytelling mode. There is possibly a lighting change to accommodate this)
We kissed momentarily, her hesitation palpable either because of something I said, her feelings for me, or the fact that she was married, although that subject never came up.

She asked, "Do I love you?" a perfectly reasonable question at the time. Looking back on it, it seems an odd thing to ask. "Do I love you?" Why would you ask that of someone else? The answer seems so completely reliant on the asker that respondent need not be involved. The asking is extraneous. But when she asked, I didn't hesitate with the answer. What was the answer...? I do remember that I had some inside information, that I was comfortable with the asking and not afraid of the answer. I knew something about her emotions that she did not. Why?

Her legs spread wide and my mind willed her hands to cuff mine at the wrists, stroking her thighs with my fingertips. Another twitch of the sleeping lip muscles and she thrust herself upon me, her skirt now riding high upon her hips while she sat longingly at the window some feet from me. I had to pee.

(He falls out of storytelling mode and back to his own neuroses) Why! Why, in the middle of a fucking fantastic dream do I have to fucking pee?! God

damnit! So, of course, I walk over to the dresser and piss in the drawer while she strokes my back. There's a fucking lake of piss in that drawer and yet everything's perfectly normal!

(During that last sentence, ROGER enters slowly, looking around the park unaware of ARTHUR. ARTHUR notices him and stops talking. ROGER then notices ARTHUR and crosses to him, hand outstretched)

ROGER
Hey there, Arthur!

ARTHUR
(immediately, almost overlapping) I had a dream about your wife, Roger.

Blackout

Valerie Borey
3744 Park Ave S
Minneapolis, MN 55407
(612) 922-9114
vborey@hotmail.com

Valerie Borey is a playwright, teacher, and researcher based in the Twin Cities. Other writings include plays such as *Mississippi Running* (2006), *Just So, Mississippi* (2007), and *The Harriet Carter Catalogue* (2008), and short fiction such as, *Beulah's Wet Pants* (Diddle Dog, 2006), *Sniffing Fumes* (American Nerd Magazine, 2006), and *You Left Bones in the Raspberry Pudding, Brother* (Heavy Glow 2008). Valerie previously served as a Company Member of Workhouse Theatre, wearing a variety of hats (dramaturg, stage manager, actor, costume designer, producer, and grant writer, at various times) and has since gone free range, focusing efforts on juggling a variety of independent projects (from constructing a Nordic themed ice shanty to writing curriculum).

Valerie graduated Phi Beta Kappa from the University of Minnesota, where she studied Cultural Anthropology, and received an M.A. in the Social Sciences from the University of Chicago. Her interests include second language acquisition, creative play and the everyday performance of ethnicity, as well as transformation through the performing arts. Her work has appeared in Learning Languages Journal (National Network for Early Language Learning), Viking Magazine, and Norwegian-American Weekly, and in edited volumes including *Children Under Construction: Critical Essays on Play as Curriculum* (Peter Lang); *Global Language, Culture, and Community* (In press); and *Developing Classroom Materials for Less Commonly Taught Languages* (Center for Advanced Research in Language Acquisition). Valerie was also a contributor to the *Standards for Learning Scandinavian Languages* (Center for European Studies, University of WI).

BEDTIME STORY
By Valerie Borey

CHARACTERS
CINDY- A young, single, attractive woman who lives alone
BRYAN- A somewhat older, married man with children
FEMALE VOICE (DORIS)- Bryan's wife

TIME/SETTING

Evening. Split scene: Cindy is in her apartment living room; Bryan is in his hobby room. They are speaking with one another on the telephone.

CINDY
Dad?

BRYAN
Who is this?

CINDY
It's me. Cindy.

BRYAN
Who?

CINDY
Dad.

BRYAN
I'm sorry. You must have the wrong number.

CINDY
No. Dad, it's okay. I know.

BRYAN
What number are you trying to reach?

CINDY
Dad. It's okay. I don't care. I won't tell anybody. Nobody would believe me anyways. What would I say, 'My dad faked his own death?' Seriously.

BRYAN
What?

CINDY
I won't tell anyone. I swear. I just knew it couldn't be true. It didn't make sense.

BRYAN
I'm really sorry, but..

CINDY
No. Don't be sorry. You know, at first, when I read your obituary in the paper, of course I thought it was true. But then, it just didn't feel right, you know. I had this feeling that you were somehow still around.

BRYAN
Cindy, you said? Listen, Cindy..

CINDY
At first, I had this weird, illogical thought that maybe your ghost was still around, you know, hovering over me. It was sort of a sensual thing, like, I could feel your presence around me. I was starting to think, that I was fantasizing about this absent father figure… And that's when I realized - my breasts were literally heaving - of course! It doesn't feel like he's dead, because he's NOT dead.

BRYAN
Your breasts were.. I'm sorry. I'm not your dad.

CINDY
That's fine. I won't call you that. What do you want me to call you?

BRYAN
Wh..My name is Bryan.

CINDY
Really? You just picked your middle name? Okay, Bryan..

BRYAN
No, really.

CINDY
I'll play along. Bryan. I'll just have to get used to it. Bryan. I'm so glad you picked

up. I said to myself that I would just try one more time. And there you go. Just when I was going to put the phone down and go wrap a leather belt around my neck, you picked up. God. Just think if you hadn't answered.

BRYAN
But..I'm sorry, I don't mean to make…so..you were going to asphyxiate yourself…

CINDY
It's been really hard on me since you -- disappeared. There I am, sitting in the park one day, reading the paper, and I see your face staring up at me from the obituaries. You didn't even have your eyes open in the picture. Did you know that?

BRYAN
But..you were going to asphyxiate yourself, you said, with a leather belt, your breasts were heaving. And then what?

CINDY
And after all those years of not talking…I guess I always just figured that the time would come when we would, as they say, make amends and put it all behind us. But then I see this obituary and, I can't even tell you, what was running through my mind.

FEMALE VOICE (In background)
Who is it?

CINDY
Who's that?

BRYAN
Nothing – hold on a sec.

FEMALE VOICE
Bryan? Who you talking to?

BRYAN
Nobody. I'll be right in..

FEMALE VOICE
What are you doing in there?

BRYAN
Just polishing my swords.

FEMALE VOICE
Well. hurry up.

BRYAN
Yes, honey. Be right there.

CINDY
Bryan? Are you talking to somebody?

BRYAN
What? No. Just...keep talking to me, baby.

CINDY
I suddenly feel just icy cold. I'm shivering! Da – Bryan... I wish you were here right now. I'd just throw myself into your arms and you could keep me warm and protect me. I'm sorry about everything. I really am.

BRYAN
You're cold.. Do you have goose pimples? Is it because you're excited?

CINDY
It's weird. It's like, what, eighty some degrees out and I'm just shivering. I'm just in my nightie, though. Maybe I should throw something else on.

BRYAN
No...don't go. You're in your nightie, huh?

CINDY
Oh, it's not the flannel one you gave me for Christmas that year. Wait, or was that Grandma? No, that was Grandma. This is just like a little...uh...just one of those little silky black camisoles with lace trim. It's really cute, actually.

BRYAN
Sounds really nice. So...you're all alone right now?

CINDY
All by my lonesome. Just sitting here, in the dark – well, no, that's not true. I lit a candle so I could see. Just sitting on the couch, with a glass of wine and a leather belt to keep me company. I was looking out at the moon and just thinking how it looks like this great big cream cake in the sky, like a big hole in the sky, and how alone it is up there. You know mom died last year?

BRYAN
Who? I mean, no.. no, I didn't.

CINDY
It was terrible. She didn't even look like herself…her skin was all shriveled, her hair started falling out, her toenails were just..

BRYAN
Let not talk about that, Cindy. Let's not talk about your mother. Tell me about you. What do you look like now, Cindy? Describe yourself to me.

CINDY
Da..Bryan! Quit. You're embarrassing me.

BRYAN
Don't be embarrassed. Tell me what you're doing. Are you lying down on the couch?

CINDY
Fine. I'll do it, but then you have to tell me afterwards. You know, why you did it, faked your own death.

BRYAN
'kay…just tell me about you right now.

CINDY
All right. I'm sitting cross-legged on the couch, in my nightie, and I'm still freezing.

BRYAN
Are your nipples hard?

CINDY
You know, I'm grown up now. It's not cute to ask me questions like that anymore. If you ever said something like that in front of my friends, I'd kill you for real.

BRYAN
Keep going.

CINDY
I dyed my hair blonde. It's shoulder length now.

BRYAN
What else..

CINDY
I don't know. I painted my nails yesterday. Uh...it's kind of a darker plum...I think the name of the color is something like, 'burgeoning blossom.'

BRYAN
Nice. What are you doing with the belt? Pick it up. Tell me what you were about to do with it.

CINDY
(Sighs) This reminds me of the time you caught me smoking and made me smoke the rest of the pack while you sat there and watched.

BRYAN
Pretend I'm sitting there right now and watching. Tell me what you were about to do with the belt.

CINDY
You okay? You sound funny.

BRYAN
Keep going.

CINDY
I was going to put it around my neck…

BRYAN
Put it around your neck right now.

CINDY
Daddy!

BRYAN
Don't call me that….wait...that's okay. You can call me Daddy.

CINDY
Really? 'kay. It doesn't feel right to call you Bryan….Okay.

BRYAN
Okay, it's around your neck? Pull it tight, so that you can feel the buckle biting into

                your skin.

                CINDY
                Okay.

            FEMALE VOICE
      Bryan? Are you coming or what?

                BRYAN
     Fuck off! I'll come when I come, dammit.

                CINDY
        Who's there with you?

                BRYAN
No one. That's just the TV. Okay, Cindy. Are you still on the couch? Were you going to tie the belt to something? Go ahead and tie it to something.

                CINDY
There's the coffee table, I guess. But I'll have to get down on the floor.

                BRYAN
    Just do it. Tell me when you're on the floor.

                CINDY
Okay. I'm on the floor. I can't really tie it to the leg, but I can put the leg on top of it.

                BRYAN
      Okay, tell me when you're done.

                CINDY
Okay, Daddy. I'm done. How you are you going to punish me this time?

                BRYAN
I want you to close your eyes and imagine me on top of you, pushing up your nightie—

                CINDY
                What?

                BRYAN
     And touching your cunt with my –

CINDY
What? Eew! That's sick. You sick mother fucker. What the fuck is your problem? That's disgusting!

BRYAN
What? You called me.

CINDY
What the fuck? You're not even my dad, are you?

BRYAN
Of course I'm not your dad. Why would you think I'm your dad? What kind of a sick family do you come from?

CINDY
What? You think I called you to..

BRYAN
You called me so you could pretend to talk dirty to your old man. Isn't that what you wanted?

CINDY
Eeew. I'm going to puke.

FEMALE VOICE
Bryan! The kids won't go the bed until you read them their story. I don't know what you're doing in there, but this is the last –

BRYAN
I'm coming, Doris. Okay, I'm coming.

(Click. Phone goes dead.)

CINDY
Wait, Dad…. I'm sorry. Is it really you? Daddy?

(Blackout.)

Halitosis
By Roger Brookfield

Roger Brookfield
3622 Meadow Avenue
Cheviot Ohio 45211
513-662-3937
unfunnyoldguy@yahoo.com

Roger Brookfield has had plays staged or given readings in Madison & Milwaukee WI, Austin TX, Los Angeles, and Springfield and Cincinnati OH.

Roger Brookfield (Cheviot, OH), a graduate of the University of Wisconsin (Milwaukee), with post-graduate studies at the University of Texas (Austin), is an original member of CPI, with staged readings in each of CPI's 12 seasons. He had plays performed in Madison and Milwaukee, WI; Austin, TX; Springfield and Cincinnati, OH; and Los Angeles, CA. Brookfield was twice among finalists at the 1st Stage LA's national One-Act Contest.

CHARACTERS
TELLER: Female
ROBBER: Male or can be Female

SETTING
The teller's window at a bank.

(Lights up to reveal the TELLER at her window. ROBBER enters.)

TELLER
May I help you?

ROBBER
Yeah, okay, look, no talking, don't push the alarm, don't do nothin' stupid. Just fill up the bag with what you got in the drawer an' nobody'll get hurt—Hey! Just fill up the bag—what're you—I told you nobody'd get hurt—What're you, crying?

TELLER
No, my eyes are watering. What'd you eat?

ROBBER
What'd I eat? What do you care?

TELLER
Because—God! Hey, I don't know what you've got there, what you're hiding, if you're carrying a gun—Whatever. But believe me, you don't need a gun or anything. Your breath would stop a truck.

ROBBER
Whaaat!

TELLER
No, please! Please! Please. Don't do that. Please keep your mouth shut. God! Don't you brush? Have you ever heard of toothpaste? Eewww, I think I'm gonna be sick right here on the floor. And I'm gonna have to walk in it.

You're gonna make me have to walk in it! God, what'd you do, swallow a toilet?

ROBBER
Hey, don't be pullin' no gettin' sick with me. Just fill the bag.

TELLER
Then go stand over there.

ROBBER
Over where?

TELLER
Over there.

ROBBER
Hey, I ain't standin' nowhere but here and you better start fillin' that bag.

TELLER
Then I'm not gonna open the drawer. Bad enough I might puke on the floor-- Or on you! But if I puke in the drawer? They'll have my job! Who wants to have to reach in the drawer and take out all those soggy bills? Eewww! You'd have to clean off each one of them before you could use them again.

ROBBER
Nobody'd have to clean 'em off.

TELLER
What would you do, use bills with puke all over them?

ROBBER
I don't care! Now just do what I told ya!

TELLER
I can't! Oh God, here it comes—

(She claps a hand to her mouth.)

ROBBER
Hey, wait, wait, wait, don't do that, don't to that . . . Here. Here's what I'll do, okay? I'll shut my mouth. Okay? I'll shut my mouth and you can fill the bag and I'll be outa here. Okay?

(ROBBER shuts his mouth. When he tries to speak, he sounds like the Tin Man in <u>The Wizard of Oz</u>.)

ROBBER
All right, now fill up the bag.

TELLER
Hunh?

ROBBER
You heard me! Whatsamatter with you? Don't you understand English? Go on, move! Fill up the bag!

TELLER
I didn't get a thing you said.

(ROBBER opens his mouth)

ROBBER
Fill up the Goddamn bag!

TELLER
Shh! Not so loud. You want me to get in trouble? And shut your mouth. I feel like I'm gonna—

ROBBER
All right, all right, all right.

(ROBBER closes his mouth.)

ROBBER
(through closed mouth)
Now do it! Put the money in the bag!

TELLER
Now . . . Do it? Right? Now do it? Put the—something—I didn't get all of it--

ROBBER
(mouth open)
For Christ sake!

TELLER
Shhhh! You want me to throw up all over you? Shut your mouth.

(ROBBER shuts up.)

TELLER
I want to help you, I really do, but if you can't keep your mouth shut--

ROBBER
(Through closed mouth)
Then put the money in the bag!

TELLER
Then put the . . . money? Hunh? Yeah? The money . . . In the--

ROBBER
(Mouth open)
God dammit!

TELLER
No, no, that's not gonna work; I can't understand what you're saying—

ROBBER
Jesus Christ, come on!

TELLER
And keep your mouth shut! You know what? You really need something for your mouth—you could get arrested out there. You know what you could do? Suck on a lemon. Really. Suck on a lemon. Or lemon-flavored candy, how 'bout that? Or lemon-flavored sparkling water? — Oops, no, you'd drink that.

ROBBER
Are you gonna--

TELLER
Or, here, an apple. Put that in your mouth. Rinses your mouth out. Or— Here, give that one back. You didn't take a bite of it, did you? Good.

ROBBER
Lady!

TELLER

You know what I do? I chew on a stick of cinnamon gum. Works like a charm. I can have a hamburger with onions an' all, and chew a stick of cinnamon gum afterward and . . . Supercalafragilistic no more halitosis. Just one stick of cinnamon inhibits my neurosis.

ROBBER
Are you crazy?

TELLER
I don't know. But at least my breath doesn't stink.

ROBBER
Yaaaahhh!

(ROBBER races off.)

BLACKOUT

END OF PLAY

'MR. GINGERSNAP'
by:
Nichole Carey
Mossyroses11@hotmail.com

Nichole Carey: Originally from Brainerd MN, Nichole moved to the Twin Cities in 2004 to go to school and begin her career in the arts. Graduating with her BA in theatre from Metropolitan State University four years later, she has become a jack of all trades and a master of none. While her focus has been in performance the last few years, she couldn't be happier to now be creating written work for the stage. This will be her second professionally produced short play. She has also been writing and developing a full length ensemble comedy for over a year now, and is hoping to direct and produce it in conjunction with Transllusion Theatre, a new company in the area that she is currently apart of and helped found. In addition to her written work, she is also an avid vocalist, having just completed a five week musical theatre intensive under the tutelage of AMDA graduate Kathleen Bloom and piano aficionado Stephen Dewey. She has performed with such local companies as Theatre on the Park, Performing Arts Ministries, St. Paul Vintage Players, and soon can be seen in the new musical "The Silent Room" at the MN Fringe Festival, produced by New Proletkult Theatre. She would like to dedicate her play to some very special people in her life; her mother Joan, her always supportive and ever adoring husband Andrew, and her fat and fluffy tabby cat Murray, her very own soul kitty, who was the inspiration for Mr. Gingersnap.

Cast of Characters:
VIOLET: A lovely woman of any age between mid twenty's to mid forties. A very hip and modern kinda chick.

JAKE: VIOLET'S date for the evening. He should be close to her in age. An every guy type of guy, he is hoping to make it to at least second base tonight.

MR. GINGERSNAP: VIOLET's overweight cat

SETTING: VIOLET'S apt. The stage can be dressed very sparse, with even just cubes standing as a couch, chairs, etc at the director's discretion. VIOLET and JAKE enter from stage left. They stand at the lip of the stage. A spotlight comes up on them but leaves the rest of the stage black. They are hugging and definitely "clicking".

JAKE:
I had a really nice time tonight.

VIOLET: *(sincere)*
Yeah, so did I.

JAKE:
So…would it be ok if I called you again sometime?

VIOLET:
I think I'd like that.

JAKE:
Sometime soon?

VIOLET:
Even better.

JAKE:
Great. Well, looking forward to it!

VIOLET:
Me too.

JAKE:

So….can I kiss you goodnight?

VIOLET:
I don't know, can you?

JAKE:
Only one way to find out.
(They share a sweet little kiss on the lips)

JAKE:
Well, I should go.

VIOLET:
Yeah, you probably should….
(They regard each other for a moment with longing).

VIOLET:
Unless…

JAKE:
Yeah?!

VIOLET:
I mean, you could at least come in for a *little* drink.

JAKE:
I love little drinks!

VIOLET:
Oh great!

(She turns from him and looks in her purse for her keys. Jake looks up at the heavens and mouths "thank you" to the universe for his happy fate.)

VIOLET:
There they are! Sorry, this thing is like a bottomless pit sometimes.

JAKE:
No problem.

(She takes out her keys and mimes as if putting them in a door and then opening it. They step into the apt and the rest of the stage is lit up)

VIOLET:
Sorry about the mess. *(There should be no mess)*

JAKE:
Oh no this place is great. Spacious. Do you live here all by yourself?

VIOLET:
Yeah, just me, and my big fat cat Mr. Gingersnap.

JAKE:
Oh, you have a cat?

VIOLET:
Oh no, are you allergic? So many guys are allergic to cats nowadays.

JAKE:
Oh no! I love cats! Especially ones named after desserts

VIOLET:
Yeah I know, but I thought about changing it, but figured it might mess with him too much. New home and new name all in one day?

JAKE:
Well, where is the big guy?

VIOLET:
He should be around her somewhere. He likes to sleep under my bed. Mr. Gingersnap! Mommy's home!

(A rather large and grotesque man in some sweats enters from stage right. He is also wearing a collar with a bell on it. He is yawning and scratching his belly. To VIOLET and JAKE, he is a cat)

VIOLET:
There's my big boy! Did you miss your mommy? You sure did didn't you?
*(she goes over to him. He
sees her and drops to the floor and joyously mews and rubs up around her legs
as she pets him)*

JAKE:
Hey there Mr. Gingersnap

(He moves to them and tries to pet MR. GINGERSNAP. He sees him and hisses and scratches angrily at JAKE. He nips JAKE and he pulls back)

JAKE:
OW!

VIOLET:
Oh Jake I'm sorry! I should have warned you, he can get a little aggressive around strange men. Did he get you bad?

JAKE:
I think I'll live.

VIOLET:
Yeah, *(she goes to MR. GINGERSNAP who is in a ball and growling at JAKE)* I got him at a shelter a few months ago. *(She begins to pet MR. GINGERSNAP and he slowly begins to unfurl and once again lovingly start to rub against her)* I know he's a little older, but I didn't want a kitten. We looked into each other's eyes, and I just knew I had to bring him home.

JAKE:
Well he certainly seems to have taken to you.

VIOLET:
I know right?! It's like he's always been mine. I think he's my soul kitty.

(as VIOLET and JAKE continue the conversation, they eventually should move away from MG and over to the couch. MR. GINGERSNAP doesn't realize at first, but then notices that no one is petting him any longer. He is annoyed)

JAKE:
Yeah, I had one of those once.

VIOLET:
You did?

JAKE:
He was my old farm cat named Pickles.

VIOLET:
Pickles!?

JAKE:

Yeah. My mom and dad liked to can a lot and the summer I turned ten we got this little calico kitten. We canned more pickles that summer than I can remember, so the name seemed to fit.

VIOLET:
So you grew up on a farm?

JAKE:
No, just far enough out of the city that we could have a garden bigger than a sandbox.
(MR. GINGERSNAP regards them, and finally makes his way over to the couch as they flirt. He is still on the floor, but sits down right between them. He begins to bathe himself.)

VIOLET:
So do you have a green thumb would you say?

JAKE:
Not any greener than yours.

(He takes her hand and looks at her thumb. He is trying to be sexy, but he keeps noticing MR. GINGERSNAP, who is now trying to lick himself in his private area. This starts to make JAKE very uncomfortable after a while)

VIOLET:
Well, that must not be very much then because I kill plants so much as look at them!

JAKE: *(Laughing)*
You do? *(Trying not to notice MR. GINGERSANP, who is only getting more graphic)*

VIOLET:
Yeah, I can't even keep my rock garden alive!

JAKE:
Is that so?... *(he is staring at MR. GINGERSNAP)*

VIOLET:
Um...are you ok?

JAKE:
I don't mean to be weird but, your cat is kind of freaking me out.

(She looks down at MR. GINGERSNAP)

VIOLET:
Oh! Mr. Gingersnap you stop that!

(She bats at him and he recoils hissing)

VIOLET: I'm so sorry.

JAKE:
No- I mean, I didn't mean to make a big deal out of it.

VIOLET:
No, I'm glad you said something. He shouldn't be doing that around polite company.

JAKE:
Well, *(moving closer to her)* who said anything about me being polite?
(MR. GINGRESANP notices and gets upset)

VIOLET:
Oh, you don't look like such a bad boy to me.

JAKE:
Well, I can surprise you

VIOLET:
Oh really?
(Jake moves in for another kiss. Suddenly MR. GINGERSNAP makes a decision and in a great attempt jumps up on the couch and gets between JAKE and VIOLET. He faces VIOLET and makes every effort to put his ass in JAKES face as much as he can.)

VIOLET:
Oh Mr. Gingersnap! What are doing? Sorry Jake

JAKE:
No, no that's fine.

VIOLET:
I guess he must be jealous- isn't that cute?

JAKE:

Oh yeah…adorable.

VIOLET:
You are just so starved for love aren't you Mr. Gingersnap?
(MR. GINGERSNAP lays out on his back across both of them)

Oh, do you want your belly rubbed?

(She begins to rub his belly. He stretches out across them luxuriously)

VIOLET:
Isn't he just the greatest cat ever?

JAKE:
Yeah… great.

VIOLET:
You can rub his belly Jake- he won't scratch you again, I promise.

JAKE:
Well…

VIOLET:
Oh come on just look at him!!!

JAKE:
Uh… *(trying to get the evening back under control)* weren't we going to have a drink?
(He manages to push MR. GINGERSNAP off of their laps. He rolls heavily back onto the stage. He lays there perturbed.

VIOLET:
Oh that's right! *(She stands up)* would you like a glass of wine or something stronger?

JAKE:
Well, whatever you've got I think I can handle.

VIOLET:
We'll see about that. *(she exits the stage)*

(JAKE takes off his suit coat and starts to make himself comfortable. MR.

GINGERSNAP approaches him slowly)

JAKE:
Nice kitty…now you just go make some hair balls some place else tonight ok? You might not want to see what I'm going to do to your "mommy"

(Suddenly, MR. GINGERSNAP stands up straight and confronts JAKE)

MR GINGERSNAP:
Get the fuck out.

JAKE:
What the-

MR: GINGERSNAP:
You heard me- now get the fuck out.

JAKE:
Are you… *talking* to me?

MR GINGERSNAP:
Look asshole, I've got a good thing going on here with Violet. I'm not going to let some jerk in a cheap Armani knock off ruin it for me this early in the game, so get the fuck out before I turn your face into a bowl of chef Boyardee. Ka peesh?

JAKE:
Are you serious?!...

VIOLET
: Hope you like whiskey sours…

(VIOLET reenters with two glasses. Mr. GINGERSNAP drops to the floor and rolls onto his back in a submissive gesture)

VIOLET:
Ah! I told you he was a sweetie! See, he likes you.

JAKE:
Uh…. *(not quite sure what to make of things)*

VIOLET:
Come on, I bet we'll enjoy these more in the bedroom…

(she begins to move off stage.)

JAKE:
Uh…

(Mr. Gingersnap gets up to his knees and draws his hand across his neck in a threatening gesture at JAKE.)

JAKE:
Violet I gotta go.

VIOLET:
What?! Why?

JAKE:
(He moves and speaks quickly) I am allergic to cats. I forgot. My head feels like it's about to explode. Sinus's… pounding…I should just go.

VIOLET:
But Jake!

JAKE:
(he kisses he brusquely on the cheek) Sorry, take care of yourself, give me a call sometime you ever get rid of your cat.

VIOLET:
But…

JAKE:
See ya Violet. *(He stops and turns back for a moment before he leaves)* Bye Mr. Gingersnap sir. *(He exits)*

(pause)

VIOLET:
Well God damn it! That is the third guy in less than a month that has just fled this apartment.
(she makes her way over to the couch)

I just don't know what I keep doing so wrong.

(MR. GINGERSNAP makes his way over to her and jumps up onto the couch

and lays across her lap once again)

VIOLET:
At least I know I'll always have you Mr. Gingersnap. *(She begins to pet him)* My one true love.

(MR. GINGERSNAP stretches and gives a long satisfied sigh and a long satisfied fart)

VIOLET:
(laughing) Oh Mr. Gingersnap!

(She continues to pet him as the lights fade to black)

Wingman

By Eric "Pogi" Sumangil
pogmyster@gmail.com

Over the last decade, Eric "Pogi" Sumangil has been one of the most often-mispronounced names in the Twin Cities theater community. Go ahead, try it. We double dog dare you. He is a two-time recipient of the Jerome Foundation's Many Voices Fellowship at The Playwrights' Center, and still sleeps with the Pound Puppy he got when he was 8, cleverly named Puppy.

His breakout performance was the role of Papa Bear in The Trial of Goldilocks in 8th grade. Since then he's gone on to work with The Children's Theater, Mu Performing Arts, Mixed Blood Theatre Company, Mo'olelo Performing Arts, Eye of the Storm Theater, Chanhassen Dinner Theatres, Frank Theater, The History Theater, La Jolla Playhouse, The Ordway Center, and The Guthrie Theater among others.

He is a proud member of Actors' Equity Association, and the 2002 recipient of the Fil-Minnesotan Association Excellence in the Arts Award, as well as the distinguished Beefeater award for eating a three-pound steak in under an hour at a steakhouse in Illinois. Seriously, there's a plaque and everything.

A row of chairs facing the audience. Ideally, each of the chairs would be filled by actors except two next to each other. The two empty chairs should not be directly center stage.

At rise, each of the actors are in their chairs as if they are waiting for a performance to begin. CECE, 24, and JAYAR, 23, enter hurriedly through the entrance to the theater and look around. They find the two open seats in the "audience".

They speak sotto voce, so as to not disturb the "play"

NOTE to JAYAR: All the silences should be outside the comfort zone for any normal play. I'm talking at least 30 seconds to a minute or more. Also, any reactions from the audience (coughing, fidgeting, and especially laughter) should pique your interest as if something is about to happen or just happened on stage.

NOTE to CECE: Feel free to apologize to people around you if JAYAR begins to speak in a way that would otherwise bother people trying to watch a play.

JAYAR
[taking off his coat]
Did it start already?

CECE
I think it just started.

They sit and watch silently for an uncomfortably long time. JAYAR flips through his program, looking up occasionally. Finally:

JAYAR
So which one is she?

CECE
She's not on stage yet.

Another long silence.

JAYAR
They're not doing anything.

Silence.

JAYAR*
Well, at least they got food.

JAYAR eats through the next long pause.

JAYAR
What the fuck, dude? What the hell is this? [beat] This chick better be fuckin' hot, dude, cuz this is some bullshit.

CECE
Shut up, dude. I went to that Sarah Palin book-signing with you so you could stand in line with what's-her-name.

JAYAR
What can I say, dude? I feel it's my responsibility as a man of the new millennium to help the hot, uptight, sexually-repressed conservatives get in touch with their freaky sides.

CECE shushes JAYAR.

JAYAR concedes but continues to pout through the next long silence. When his boredom finally gets the best of him:

JAYAR
[disguised as a cough]
Bullshit!

CECE nudges JAYAR's elbow. JAYAR returns the gesture. Another long silence.

JAYAR
Are you sure all these people are actors? I'm better looking than half the guys up there, maybe I should be an actor.

CECE
Dude, shut up.

JAYAR

Check out those two over there. You think they're supposed to be married? On a date? You said your chick's not up there. What if she had to kiss a dude in a play?

CECE shrugs his shoulders.

JAYAR
That wouldn't bug you?

CECE
No.

JAYAR
What if she had to kiss that dude? That dude could totally take you.

CECE sighs audibly.

JAYAR
Oooh, hola mamasita. She's pretty cute. Maybe I'll walk away from this with a date, too.

JAYAR winks at the girl and blows a couple of kisses at her. More silence.

JAYAR
So is this, like, one of those fringe things?

CECE
No.

JAYAR
Oh.

Silence.

JAYAR
Ok, so I don't get this—

CECE
Dude, just shut up and watch the play.

JAYAR
Watch what? They're not doing anything. They're just sitting there. I bet you can't even explain what this shit is about.

CECE
It's like, a commentary on how... we're always being watched... like, in our society... voyeurism and shit.

JAYAR
[after a beat]
That's the gayest shit I've ever heard.

CECE
What the fuck, dude?

JAYAR
[turning to the person on the other side of him]
Excuse me, can you tell me what's going on? Sorry, I don't usually see shit, I mean, things like this so maybe I'm missing—

CECE
[Speaking across JAYAR to the person on the other side of him]
I'm really sorry. He's... tourettes. [to JAYAR] Why does everything have to be a big fucking production with you?

JAYAR locks eyes with CECE for a moment, then without any warning, JAYAR jumps up onto his chair.

JAYAR
Excuse me, can anyone tell me what your show is about?

CECE
Dude!

JAYAR
Is this a big enough production for you? OK, so what is this about?

JAYAR gets an answer from an audience member. CECE hides his face with his hand.

During the section that follows, JAYAR goes around the audience and tries to make connections between the "characters" by asking questions like (but not limited to) the following:

Are you one of the leads?

Is this a musical? [get the audience member to sing something]

So are you one of the good guys or one of the bad guys?

Who's, like, your archenemy?

Do you guys know each other?

By a show of hands, how many of you guys could kick this guy's ass?

What clan do you belong to?
[to audience] How many other people up here are members of his clan?
What is your clan's battle cry?

Ideally the goal is to come up with a story, from beginning to end, that links all the "characters" together. JAYAR then goes back to his chair, and tells the story in its entirety to CECE, who sits mortified. After all is said and done:

JAYAR
…and that's what this show is about.

CECE
[whispers]
Thanks.

JAYAR
Huh?

CECE
[full voice]
Thank you.

JAYAR
[Shushes him then silently mouths the words]
They're doing a play.

They sit in silence and watch the audience for a few more beats.

JAYAR
See dude, I totally get this now.

*This line may be omitted if it doesn't fit with the standard goings on at the theater/venue

Mame Pelletier
mamepelletier@gmail.com

Flapjacks and Bagels

Mame Pelletier is an actor/writer/improviser/comedian and now playwright based out of Saint Paul, MN. She spent most of her formative teenage years in the Twin Cities, and most of her formative adult life in the Northwestern United States. She graduated cum laude with a BFA from the University of Oregon.

Flapjacks and Bagels was adapted from a radio sketch written for the variety radio show *LiveWire!,* based out of Portland, OR. Mame was a staff writer and vocal artist for *LiveWire!* for two and a half years, until she moved back to Minnesota. Mame spends most of her creative energy performing on various stages around the Twin Cities, and is looking forward to putting more ink to the page.

Mame is thrilled to have her first play being produced by *Freshwater Theatre Co.*, a company she not only loves, but to which she also belongs. She would like to dedicate this play to her boy David, with whom she was pregnant when the idea was originally conceived. (see what she did there?)

Characters:
Jill – boss, 4 months pregnant/first baby
Carl – guy's guy/father
Brenda – suburban mom
Juan – new-ageish father

Office meeting-room setting. A table, projector, and table with party goodies are in the room. Also, there's a smattering of sad holiday decorations around the room and possible Christmas Sweaters on the people. All but Jill are seated. Lights halfway up.

JILL:
…which is why Rick truly believes this new sales initiative will bring prosperity and growth to Clovernut, Incorporated.

Jill covers the projector with a paper, or turns off the light.

And, with that, my presentation's done and it's just about time for the party! Before we dive into the eggnog and cookies, I'd like to take a couple minutes for questions on the initiative if you have any.

Jill turns on the lights.

CARL:
Uh, yeah. Umm a couple of us were wondering if you're pregnant or just gaining holiday weight?

JILL:
Uh. Wow. I was going to make an official announcement after the holidays. But… I guess now is as good a time as any! Keep that eggnog virgin for this gal! I've got a bun in the ol' oven!

BRENDA:
Congrats! Speaking of old ovens, did you have to do IVF?

JUAN:
Oh! Does that mean you're having twins?

JILL:
No, I'm not having twins, why would you… never mind.

CARL:
Speaking of *virgins*, it's obviously not an immaculate conception. Did you see her at last year's holiday party?

JILL:
Excuse me?

CARL:
Nothing.

JILL:
Look, does anybody have a question about my presentation?

BRENDA:
Are you planning on breastfeeding exclusively? It'll take all the bounce outta your girls.

JILL:
(trying to laugh it off) I'm almost positive that's none of your business, Brenda. Thank you all for your interest in my baby, my one. tiny. naturally conceived. baby. Now seriously, are there any questions about the new sales initiative?

JUAN:
Yes, I wanted to verify that if we increase our sales 2% next quarter, we'll be placed in a drawing for a spring cruise?

JILL:
Thank you Juan. Yes that is correct, *and* good news for those that increased their sales 5% over the past year… you will find an extra 5% in your bonus!

JUAN:
Follow up question?

JILL:
Go ahead.

JUAN:
You should consider sharing a family bed, if you want your child to grow up feeling loved and supported and not at all serial-killerish.

JILL:
That's not a question.

BRENDA:
No way Juan! What is she, a hippie? Family-bed-hippies are the serial killers! She could roll over and smother his tiny little defenseless body. Oh! I said "his" – do you know if it's a boy or girl? With your fashion sense you should really have a boy.

CARL:
She's having a boy. See her gut, the way it looks all droopy and saggy? She's carrying just like my wife did and I have 3 boys – thank-you-very-much!

JUAN:
I make a great organic salve that will keep your nipples from cracking for after you start breastfeeding, which you really should do.

CARL:
Ewwww, I remember that. They were like a couple of big ol' dried out flapjacks. Get out the syrup! High five!

BRENDA:
And don't forget to do your kegels, you *and* your husband will appreciate that in the long run!

CARL:
Amen. Kegels and bagels – my favorite morning treat. The more schmear the better! Fist bump!

JUAN:
You know many cultures revere the placenta for its symbolism of life, spirit and individuality. You should keep it and bury it under a tree.

BRENDA:
Oh my gah, I heard that this British couple cooked theirs and made pate out of it and-

JILL:
THAT'S FUCKING FUCK ENOUGH!

Jill starts collecting her things and unhooking her computer

JUAN:
(*under his breath*) you really shouldn't swear in front of the baby

BRENDA:
(*under her breath*) psycho

CARL:
(*under his breath*) girl needs to chill out, once that baby comes she'll *really* be tired and stressed out

JILL:
I can hear every word you're saying.
(*in Helen Kellerspeak*) I'm pregnant, not deaf.

Beat

Jill goes back to trying to unhook her computer but has trouble with the cords

JILL:
Goddamn these cords!

JUAN:
Ahhh, the umbilical cord is a beautiful symbol of-

During the following dialogue, Juan gets the cords in order, brings them to Jill, and, by the end, can't resist touching her belly.

JILL:
OHMYGODWILLYOUPLEASESHUTUP?! My baby's umbilical cord is none of your goddamn business. And neither are my fucking nipples!

CARL:
(*interjection - titillated*) She said "fucking nipples!"

JILL:
You think you know it all?!! You think you've got the corner on tired and stressed and love?!! Do you really thing you've got all the goddamn answers?!!

All affirm.

(*trying to recompose*) I promise to come to you if I have any questions, but, until that happens, my pregnancy is no longer up for discussion. Happy Holidays. JUAN, GET YOUR GOD DAMN HANDS OFF MY BELLY!

Jill exits

Beat

BRENDA:
I wonder if she'll come back after maternity leave. I should polish up my resume.

JUAN:
The hormones of the pregnant female can make them very moody.

CARL:
Preachin' to the choir, Juan. Preaching to the choir.

Lights

STRINGS

J. Merrill Motz
justmotz@gmail.com

J. Merrill Motz, or Jeremy Motz, or just Motz (rhymes with boats) just received a graduate degree from Ohio University's Professional Playwriting Program, after having spent four years in Minneapolis, where he moved after graduating from Central Michigan University with a BFA in acting. While in the Twin Cities, he acted for Chameleon Theatre Circle, Workhouse, took classes at the Playwright's Center and The Loft, and appeared as Saul in the original production of *Table 12* in the 2010 Minnesota Fringe.

At CMU, his plays *Ain't That A Kick in the Head*, *Just One*, *Nobody Flinched Down By The Arcade,* and *The Roommate* were produced by the Alpha Psi Omega one-act festival, with *Ain't That A Kick in the Head* and *The Roommate* selected to be performed at the Kennedy Center American College Theatre Festival in 2006 and 2007. *The Roommate* was commissioned by the University of Wisconsin Fond du Lac to be developed into a full-length production for their 2008 main stage season. His full-length script, *All Gonna Go*, just received a reading from Swandive Theatre in Minneapolis. In Spring 2011, his latest script, *Reinforce Sincerity,* received a reading at the Seabury Quinn, Jr. Playwright's Festival in Athens, OH. Motz was recently published in the online crime fiction magazine Plots With Guns in March 2010, and hopes to dabble some more in crime fiction if he can ever find the time.

JEN sits alone at bar. TONY enters, a coat covering one arm. He sees her, approaches.

JEN

I don't know...should I have another? Okay, yes...I'll have another.

TONY sits next to her. She looks at him. He smiles. She looks away.

TONY

I'll have a seven and seven, thanks.

TONY glances at JEN, who ignores him. He lets the coat drop and raises WOLF PUPPET.

He places it on the bar between them.

WOLF PUPPET

Hey, hey, LI'l Red Riding Hood...do you know the way to Grandmother's House?

JEN

Why, hello, Mr. Wolf.

WOLF PUPPET

Careful, Li'l Red...I'm the Big...BAD...Wolf.

JEN

Oh, I see. Big Bad Wolf, is it?

TONY

I'm sorry. He's got a mind of his own.

JEN

I doubt that. So, you want to know the way to Grandmother's house, Mr. Big Bad Wolf?

WOLF PUPPET

Welll....her place...or yours...?

JEN

You need to work on your pick-up lines, Mr. Big Bad Wolf.

TONY removes the WOLF PUPPET from the bar and speaks directly to JEN.

TONY

Sorry, it was the best I got. Hi, I'm Tony. I'm studying puppetry.

JEN

Hi, Tony. Excuse me, I'm talking to the Big Bad Wolf...?

(Pause.)

TONY puts the puppet back on the bar.

TONY

Oh, uh, sure. Great, nice pick, Tony.

JEN

So, Mr. Big Bad Wolf...did you know Li'l Red Riding Hood actually seduced the wolf to go to her grandmother's house?

WOLF PUPPET

Why, no...I don't think I knew that...

JEN

Oh, sure. In the Brothers Grimm story, the wolf was just minding his own business when he came upon LI'l Red in the forest. It was her that told him how to get there.

WOLF PUPPET

Welllll...lucky him...

JEN

Well, sure. Until the wolf got greedy and had to eat them both. Then he was too full to move and fell asleep in Grandmother's bed. And the huntsman came by and cut open his belly and rescued Li'l Red and Grandmother and filled him up with stones instead.

WOLF PUPPET

So I...uh...shouldn't be so greedy?

JEN

Oh, the wolf couldn't help that. It was in his nature. There are lots of stories of the wolf being greedy and gluttonous. Most of them end with his belly full of stones. Is that what you want?

WOLF PUPPET

Uh...not really, no.

JEN

Then you should avoid the fox. The fox is cunning and clever, and always out to trick the wolf for being so greedy.

WOLF PUPPET

Uh...good thing there's no foxes here, right?

JEN

Well, maybe Li'l Red Riding Hood was the fox. She tricked him, didn't she? And she's red, just like a fox...

TONY

Foxes are orange.

JEN

They're orange-ish red.

TONY

Reddish orange, maybe.

JEN

Mr. Big Bad Wolf, what do you think think.

WOLF PUPPET

Uh...orange-ish red.

JEN

Good answer. See, the fox is always pulling the wolf's strings. He can't help it. Who's pulling your strings, I wonder?

WOLF PUPPET

Oh, I don't have strings. He's actually got his hand up in my--

JEN

I know, Mr. Wolf. But if I asked you whose hand is all up inside you, it would sound pretty weird, wouldn't it? Besides, I wasn't asking you.

(Pause.)

TONY

...Huh?

JEN

I'm Jen, Tony.

TONY

Oh, hi!

JEN

I'm glad to meet the both of you tonight. You're like the perfect fortune cookie you get one day too late.

WOLF PUPPET

Well, in that case, let my proctologist here buy you a drink...

JEN

No, thanks. I got a letter from home today, Mr. Wolf. E-mail, actually. And home is in Michigan, thanks for asking. It seems my...my boyfriend Adam went and got himself engaged. While I've been away out here at school. Studying...folklore and fairy tales.

TONY removes the puppet from the bar.

TONY

I'm sorry...

JEN

Shh, Tony. I'm talking to Mr. Wolf.

TONY puts the puppet back on the bar.

WOLF PUPPET

I'm sorry...

JEN

Shh. Just listen. So, Adam got engaged. News to me. I thought things were going great, long distance wise. So I wonder, is it my fault? Did I...pull his strings, like the fox, to send him away, because I'm not there? Or is he pulling my strings from there, letting me think everything's okay? And then I think, how long have I let him pull? And is he the only one? Was the long distance thing actually my idea? Was school? Was anything? Are any of my ideas mine anymore? Did I even want to come to this bar tonight, or has the idea been implanted in my head, like Grandmother's house, that this is what I need to do after I get dumped? Who put the idea in Tony's head, Mr. Wolf, that he needed you to talk to me? Who's pulling our strings, hm?

JEN pulls the puppet from TONY's hand.

TONY

Uh, I can't, um, I can't make him talk if you take him--

JEN

I know, Tony, come on.

TONY

Sorry.

JEN

I like him better this way. He seems more alive than ever, don't you, Mr. Wolf? I know. Barkeep! Some drinks for me and my two friends here! Nobody pulling our strings anymore.

TONY

Oh, thanks...but I, uh...I don't think they'll serve a puppet here...

JEN

Don't be silly, Tony. They've been serving me all night.

Old MacDonald Dirge

by
Justin Maxwell
651.238.2913
justinmaxwell75@hotmail.com
2333 Priscilla St. #10
St. Paul, MN 55108

"The limits of my language are the limits of my world."
—Ludwig Wittgenstein

Justin Maxwell's plays have been performed in Chicago, Minneapolis, and NYC. He has published prose in various journals, including *Contemporary Theatre Review*, *American Theatre*, and AWP's *Pedagogy Forum*. Justin has an MFA in creative writing from Hamline University, and is the Drama Editor of the literary journal *Midway*. He teaches at Hamline University and at Minneapolis Community and Technical College

Spotlight reveals a small, serious child, the SINGER, a soloist in some kind of grade school program complete with cheesy plywood animals and farm stuff.

The child begins sings a variation of "Old MacDonald Had a Farm." It is performed to the usual tune but done at about ¼ or so of the usual speed so that each verse takes about 30 seconds. In other words, dirge tempo. The more dirge-like the better. However, there is enough material here for an actor to modify the performance to fit their personal style. As the SINGER becomes progressively sadder as the song progresses, and is openly crying by the end. The work becomes funnier the slower and sadder it is performed—this is fun with schadenfreude.

<u>SINGER</u>
Old MacDonald had a farm
E, I, E, I, O
And on this farm he had a horse
E, I, E, I, O
And this horse it's name was puppy
E, I, E, I, O

Old MacDonald had a farm
E, I, E, I, O
And on this farm he had a cow
E, I, E, I, O
And this cow it's name was puppy
E, I, E, I, O

Old MacDonald had a farm
E, I, E, I, O
And on this farm he had a lamb
E, I, E, I, O
And this lamb it's name was puppy
E, I, E, I, O

Old MacDonald had a farm
E, I, E, I, O
And on this farm he had a pig
E, I, E, I, O
And this pig it's name was puppy
E, I, E, I, O

Old MacDonald had a farm
E, I, E, I, O
And on this farm he had a duck
E, I, E, I, O
And this duck it's name was puppy
E, I, E, I, O

Old MacDonald had a farm
E, I, E, I, O
And on this farm he had a veal calf
E, I, E, I, O
And this veal calf it's name was puppy
E, I, E, I, O

Lights down to dark.
END

Cut or Uncut
A Ten Minute Play by Neil Haven

Copyright Neil Haven 2008. All Rights Reserved.

Neil Haven is the author *of Pink Champagne, Stuck, The Playdaters , Get a Life, and Who Killed Santa? The Choose-Your-Own-Ending Musical Murder Mystery Holiday Whodunit.*, among others. His work has been seen at various theatres across the U.S. and Canada, including In Tandem Theatre and Uprooted Theatre in Milwaukee, Nevada Conservatory Theatre, The Chicago Fringe Festival, Denver's Dangerous Theatre, Hectic Theatre in Regina, Saskatchewan, The University of Wisconsin - Whitewater, and The University of Nevada, Las Vegas. *Who Killed Santa?...,* is available through Original Works Publishing. He lives in Milwaukee, Wisconsin. Pease email him at havenneil@gmail regarding inquiries about production rights.

www.neilhaven.com

Characters

4 men, 1 woman

Megan: *thirtyish*

Kenn: *thirtyish*

Doctor: *middle-aged*

Walter: *sixtyish*

Woodrow: *As old as possible*

MEGAN has just given birth, she holds the baby. Her husband KENN looks on with the DOCTOR.

MEGAN
Oh, you're so little. I thought you were much bigger.

DOCTOR
He's perfect. Everything is just the way it should be. A beautiful natural birth. Flawless. Is he to be circumcised?

MEGAN
No.

KENN
Yes.

MEGAN
What?

KENN
Of course he's getting circumcised.

MEGAN
Since when? We never talked about this.

KENN
Why not?

MEGAN
Why?

KENN
Because that's what you do. That's what I am. He should look like his daddy.

MEGAN
You've got a big scar on your ass too. Should we give him that?

KENN
Can we tell you tomorrow?

DOCTOR
I won't be available tomorrow.

KENN
Why not?

DOCTOR
I'm being circumcised. Please don't let that influence your decision.

KENN
Great.

DOCTOR
Let me see if I can get mine done tonight. I'll give you some time to talk.
(He exits.)

MEGAN
Is it really necessary?

KENN
Other kids will make fun of him. He should look like the other kids. Trust me. I've seen it.

WALTER
(Entering with flowers.)
Hello?

KENN
Hey Dad, come meet your grandson.

WALTER
Hey there, little guy. He's beautiful, Megan. Congratulations, son.

KENN
So we'll have him circumcised?

WALTER
Over my dead body!

KENN
What? Dad, I'm circumcised.

WALTER
I know. And I have been living with that guilt for two years.

KENN
...Two years?

WALTER
I read about it on the Wikipedia. It's horrible. They remove all these nerve endings. Thousands. It's like scrapin' off the taste buds!

KENN
They just take a little bit off.

WALTER
Fifteen square inches.

KENN
(Looking down.)
What?

WALTER
It's genital mutilation.

MEGAN
I don't want that!

WALTER
Damn straight.

KENN
I———I———

WALTER
I know exactly what you're feeling, Kenn. And I'm sorry, I am so frickin' sorry. I wish I could say it gets better, but it doesn't. I took a part of you away and I can't give it back.

WOODROW
(Enters with a cigar and a mylar balloon. He uses a walker, maybe an oxygen tank. He is ridiculously elderly.)
Where's my great-grandson?

MEGAN
Hi Woodrow.

WALTER
He's right here, Dad. He looks just like you.

WOODROW
All wrinkly.

MEGAN
So we're in agreement?

KENN
Yes. We will not have him circumcised.

WOODROW
What in the sam hill are you talkin' about?

KENN
Circumcision. For his...you know.

WOODROW
Of course he's getting circumcised. He's an American.

WALTER
That's not a reason.

WOODROW

Circumcised penises won World War Two. That's how we knew who the Jerries were!

WALTER
That was circumstantial.

WOODROW
Are you gettin' smart with me, boy?

WALTER
I'm not a boy.

WOODROW
You're not speakin' German either, thanks to this guy.

DOCTOR
(Walking gingerly.)
Hello? Hi, I just wanted to let you know that I've just had my operation, so I can be here tomorrow if you need me.

MEGAN
How did it go?

DOCTOR
It's infected. Please don't let that influence your decision.
(He exits.)

MEGAN
I wish we could ask him.

KENN
He's not gonna let you do it if you ask him first.

WOODROW
I'll do it.

MEGAN
No you won't.

WOODROW
Foreskin is the flag of surrender! We sacrificed for freedom!

WALTER

So he shouldn't have to! He can live free.

WOODROW
(Drops his pants.)
D-Day!

DOCTOR
(Pops head in.)
I just wanted to let you know that, while it does seem slightly easier to clean, I don't feel like a complete person anymore. Please don't let that influence your decision.

WOODROW
(Marches around with his pants down. Singing "Yankee Doodle Boy.")
"I'm a yankee doodle dandy, a yankee doodle do or die."

MEGAN
Woodrow! Shut up! Is it really easier to clean?

WALTER
I'm sure he can figure it out.

KENN
My penis is extremely easy to clean.

WALTER
That's like cutting your arm off so you can clean your armpit better.

KENN
I went to grade school with an uncircumcised kid. We kicked the crap out of him every day in gym. He always got picked last for dodgeball.

WOODROW
Ain't you never seen one? Looks like an anteater chokin' on a golf ball. He'll never be with a woman, they'll go screamin' from the room.

MEGAN
Woody, that's ridiculous. I love uncircumcised penises.

KENN
What? Hey.

WALTER
(Collapsing on the floor in tears.)
I want my foreskin back!

WOODROW
You kids these days are all soft! When we caught us some POWs, first thing Eisenhower did was drag 'em out the trench, stick a blade between their teeth and circumcise 'em, right then and there. And they thanked us. They may have been Nazis, but at least they weren't afraid a gettin' their carrots peeled.

DOCTOR
I should let you know that the cost of the procedure is included in the delivery package. Please don't let that influence——

KENN
Shut up! Shut up! Shut up! I'm the man. I'm the Dad. This is my call.

MEGAN
Like hell it is.

KENN
I have a wiener! I've had it my entire life! I get to say!

MEGAN
You've had one wiener. I've had hundreds. All of you are circumcised! You're all biased. We should get a perspective from someone who isn't circumcised.

KENN
Like who?

MEGAN
Like me. I'm the only one in the room who is not circumcised.

WALTER
You're not?

MEGAN
No.

KENN
No, she's not.

WOODROW

Communist.

MEGAN
And maybe I will be someday. But it will be my decision. If he really wants it done, he can pursue it as an adult, when he knows all the facts.

WOODROW
Facts. This country's goin' down the tubes.

KENN
You're right, babe.

WALTER
You hang on to that one, Kenn.

WOODROW
Well, what the hell, let's do mine again.

KENN
Can you do that?

WOODROW
We paid for it, he's doin' it. It's been gettin' droopy.

DOCTOR
I see no reason why not. This way please.

WOODROW
And I don't want no ether.
(WOODROW shuffles out after the DOCTOR, pants still at this ankles.)

MEGAN
Good. Now we have to talk about breast-feeding and formula.

WALTER
Four years. Minimum.

KENN
No formula.

MEGAN
I have a job. I'd have to watch what I eat for another year.

WALTER
It raises the IQ.

KENN
I've always wanted to try it.

WALTER
If you take hormones Kenn, you might lactate.

END OF PLAY

No Goat.

Ruth Virkus
216 W. 29th Street
Minneapolis, MN 55408
ruthvirkus@gmail.com

A National Merit Scholarship recipient who graduated with honors from the University of Minnesota Morris with degrees in history and theatre, **Ruth Virkus** is co-artistic director of Freshwater Theatre, and currently involved with two other fantastic theatre companies here in the cities, serving as Literary Manager for 20% Theatre Company, Twin Cities, and as part of the artistic company for Swandive Theatre. Previously, she worked for several years with The Flower Shop Project, a theatre company she founded with other graduates of the UMM theatre department.

During her time with FSP, Ruth co-wrote *Drowning in Velvet*, *Dawn's Inferno*, *Ladies A.I.D.*, *Auld Acquaintance*, *Attack of the Atomic Trash Monster's Bride*, and *The Fish, The Fruit and the Pet Coffin Maker*, all produced from 2005-2008. Her first solo writing endeavor, *Preferred by Discreet Women Everywhere*, produced in 2007, eventually begat a companion piece entitled *10:00 Bistro Caprice*, which was featured in *The Fresh Five* with 20% Theatre Company in January of 2009.

Her script *Table 12: A Play at a Wedding*, a hit at the 2010 Minnesota Fringe Festival, brought together the amazing group of people who eventually became Freshwater Theatre.

Her last script, *Desperation Panties*, was produced by Freshwater Theatre in May of 2011.

Lights up on an actor. Any actor.

<u>Actor.</u>
It's so bucolic. The trees. The dappled sun. Bucolic like the- green. And-
...
she walks. Through the dappled.
...the
...

(Off stage, whispered)
She prances, like a goat.

<u>Actor.</u>
She prances, like a goat.

...
(Off stage, whispered)
through dappled-

<u>Actor.</u>
I don't remember a goat. What goat? Are you looking at the same script?

(Off stage, whispered)
Like a goat, through dappled woodlands frolic-

<u>Actor.</u>
Like a- the fuck, you say?

looks out at the audience; realizes. A very long, tortured beat.

(*apologetically*) There was no goat. I...don't remember a...
Abruptly turns and walks out.
The lights fade jerkily and too slowly.

The End.

www.ingramcontent.com/pod-product-compliance
Lightning Source LLC
Chambersburg PA
CBHW071312060426
42444CB00034B/2037